GREAT
TAPAS

GREAT
TAPAS

THE ESSENCE OF SPAIN IN DELICIOUSLY
AUTHENTIC SNACKS AND APPETIZERS

Silvana Franco

H
HERMES
HOUSE

This edition produced by Hermes House
an imprint of
Anness Publishing Limited
Hermes House,
88-89 Blackfriars Road
London SE1 8HA

Publisher: Joanna Lorenz
Senior Cookery Editor: Linda Fraser
Designer: Sian Keogh
Photography and other styling: Patrick McLeavey
Food for photography: Jaqueline Clark
Illustrator: Madeleine David

Front Cover: Sam Stowell, Photographer; Helen Trent, Stylist;
Angela Boggiano, Home Economist

Printed in Hong Kong/China

1 3 5 7 9 10 8 6 4 2

Notes
For all recipes, quantities are given in both metric and imperial measures and, where
appropriate, measures are also given in standard cups and spoons. Follow one set, but
not a mixture because they are not interchangeable.

Standard spoon and cup measurements are level.
1 tbsp = 15ml, 1 tsp = 5ml, 1 cup = 250ml/8fl oz

Australian standard tablespoons are 20ml. Australian readers should use 3 tsp in place of
1 tbsp for measuring small quantities of gelatine, cornflour, salt etc.

Medium eggs should be used unless otherwise stated.

CONTENTS

INTRODUCTION

Tapas originated in Andalucia where the long summer days and warm summer evenings merge into one, and the people of southern Spain who gather outdoors on pavements and verandas enjoy lively conversation, a glass of chilled, golden fino sherry and a tasty snack typical of the region. The tradition of serving tapas with drinks is a custom that has spread from Spain to all the major cities of Europe and beyond. The word "tapa" actually means "lid", for in times past every glass of sherry bought in a local Spanish bar would come covered by a slice of bread topped with ham, cheese or fried black pudding to keep out the flies. Sadly, finding complimentary tapas is pretty rare these days, but instead we have vibrant bars offering a vast selection.

Mealtimes in Spain are lengthy affairs with a sizeable lunch served around two o'clock and dinner eaten at about ten in the evening. So, when hunger strikes in that long gap between meals, Spaniards head for their local tapas bar for something quick to eat and to catch up on the local gossip.

Tapas bars offer a fantastic variety of dishes, which make good use of colourful, flavoursome, home-produced ingredients such as extra virgin olive oil and vine-ripened tomatoes. Many bars offer house specialities featuring ingredients indigenous to the particular area, such as home-made blood sausage dishes or locally caught sardines.

Whatever is on offer, the surroundings are guaranteed to be informal, friendly and more often than not, pretty lively.

Since the days when tapas served as edible covers for glasses of sherry, the range of these delectable snacks has increased tremendously, but they are still ultimately designed for easy eating, so that their consumption disrupts the conversation as little as possible. Because of this, few tapas require cutlery and many of the morsels come astride chunks of bread or speared with cocktail sticks. There are, of course, exceptions to the rule. If you plan to tackle tapas, be prepared to get your fingers dirty. Peeling prawns which are swimming in a pungent garlic oil is no job for the fastidious, but the rewards are marvellous, so standing on ceremony is *de rigueur* for the dedicated tapas eater. In fact, some of the older tapas bars positively encourage the tossing aside of shellfish peelings by providing a carpet of fresh sawdust on the floor.

Although the tapas themselves are no longer included in the price of a sherry, the selection that's available in modern bars is usually quite amazing. There may be as many as fifty different types on offer, many of them displayed on the bar

Traditional tapas depend on the use of the best home-produced ingredients: chorizo, anchovies, olives and farmhouse cheese.

counter with an eye to colour. A plate of fried potatoes may have as its partner bright red pimientos, and the choice may include anything from simple fried almonds or chunks of cured sausage to a sophisticated dish of stuffed mussels.

This comprehensive collection of recipes has been put together with the home-cook in mind. The dishes are all very simple to make and none requires any specialized equipment. Many of the traditional tapas, such as *tortilla* and *patatas bravas,* are included, as well as plenty of contemporary dishes made from classic Spanish ingredients such as chorizo and pimientos. These modern dishes can very happily be served in conjunction with the traditional tapas to provide a balanced selection. Many of the tapas are based on bread or vegetables, so there is also a good choice for vegetarians. Lots of the tapas are served cold and are great for easy picnicking or barbecuing.

There are no hard and fast rules when it comes to eating and serving tapas, although portions do tend to be small and varied. Nor are there any schedules to adhere to; unlike formal meals, tapas can be enjoyed at any time of the day.

Most tapas dishes are quick and easy to prepare, and some of the best, such as stuffed olives, salted nuts, cubes of cheese and pickled capers, are virtually instant – ideal for serving as impromptu nibbles.

When serving tapas remember that, traditionally, they are not intended to be eaten as a main course meal, but rather as a small snack and accompaniment to a glass of sherry. If you do plan to serve tapas as a meal, mix and match a selection of dishes – choose one or two simple fish, meat or vegetable dishes and pair with something with sauce, or serve a crisp, fried dish to give a wealth of flavour, texture and colour. For a main meal, offer at least six different tapas to satisfy your guests' appetites.

Tapas are the perfect accompaniment to lively conversation and warm companionship. With these recipes in your repertoire, entertaining will always be a pleasure.

Friendly surroundings and a lively atmosphere typify the traditional tapas bar, where a vast array of delicious tapas are on offer.

GLOSSARY OF SPANISH FOODS

Aceite – oil
Aceituna – olive
Ajo – garlic
Albóndiga – meatball
Alioli or Aïoli – garlic mayonnaise from Catalonia
Almandras – almonds
Almejas – clams
Anchoa or *Boquerón* – anchovy
Arroz – rice
Azafran – saffron
Bacalao – salt cod
Chipirones or *chopitos* – small squid
Chorizo – pork and paprika sausage, usually cured
Gambas – prawns
Hígado – liver

Huevo – egg
Jamón – ham
Jerez – sherry
Manchego – ewe's milk cheese
Morcilla – black pudding from Asturias
Pan – bread
Patatas – potatoes
Perejil – parsley
Pescado – fish
Pollo – chicken
Queso – cheese
Salsa – sauce
Sidra – cider
Tascas – tapas bars
Tortilla – omelette
Vieiras – scallops

INGREDIENTS

BLACK PUDDING
This is an important ingredient all over Spain. Different regions have their own specialized "blood sausage" but probably the most common is *morcilla*. This is flavoured with garlic, marjoram and paprika and various other ingredients, such as coriander, chilli and red wine.

CHEESE
Manchego, made from ewe's milk, originates from La Mancha and is available in various stages of maturation. It is very difficult to find a soft and creamy young Manchego outside Spain, however, it is quite widely available from cheese shops and continental delicatessens as a tangy, full-flavoured, hard cheese.

Monte Enebro is a delicious soft goat's cheese. It has a good strong flavour without being overpowering.

Picos Blue, which comes from the Cabrales region in northern Spain, is wrapped in maple leaves.

CHORIZO
Chorizo is a pork sausage flavoured with paprika. It is readily available in a selection of shapes and sizes in both smoked and unsmoked varieties. Although it is generally sold cured and ready-to-eat, it is possible to find fresh chorizo that needs to be cooked before eating. All the recipes in this book call for the cured variety.

Clockwise from bottom left: sliced chorizo, jamón serrano, chorizo sausages and black pudding.

Full-flavoured Spanish cheeses for cooking or eating, from left: Picos Blue, Manchego and Monte Enebro.

CLAMS
Clams come in a wide range of different sizes and varieties. Small ones – a little larger than cockles, similar to the type used in the classic Italian dish *Spaghetti Vongole* – are recommended for the recipes in this book, but you can can use any type and adjust the cooking times accordingly. Prepare and cook as for mussels (see below).

GARLIC
Garlic is a popular flavouring ingredient in Spanish cooking and features prominently in a number of tapas. The amount you use is largely a matter of personal taste. There are white-skinned, pink-skinned and purple-skinned varieties – the latter is generally considered to be the best.

JAMÓN SERRANO
This delicious salt-cured ham is rosy pink in colour and is eaten raw. It is sold on delicatessen counters, cut into paper-thin slices. Other cured hams which can be used instead include Italian Parma ham, or prosciutto, and Belgian *Jambon d'Ardennes*.

MUSSELS
Whenever possible, choose fresh live mussels. Soak them in cold water for about 1 hour before cooking and always use on the day of purchase. Scrape off any barnacles with a round-bladed knife, then pull out any gritty beards still attached to the mussels. Before cooking, sharply tap any open mussels with a knife and discard any that don't close immediately. To simply steam the mussels, place them in a large covered pan with a splash of wine or water, cover and cook for 2–5 minutes, depending upon the size, until all the shells have opened. Mussels are naturally salty, so do not add any extra. Discard any mussels that remain closed.

It is often said that mussels should never be cooked twice, and it is true that there is nothing worse than an over-cooked, soggy mussel that is starting to disintegrate, but provided they are not initially over-done, they can happily be added to other dishes such as *paella* or briefly cooked again, as in the mouthwatering Grilled Mussels with Parsley and Parmesanon page 34.

OLIVES
All the olives we see in stores have been cured, as they are not edible straight from the tree. Where possible, choose olives with their stones in and pit them yourself. It is preferable to buy them loose in brine rather than packed in oil; keep them in the fridge and use within a few days.

PAPRIKA
This is a very popular seasoning made from ground red pepper. It is very mild and can be used generously to add flavour and vibrant colour to many Spanish dishes.

ROASTED PEPPERS
Roasted peppers are more often cooked under the grill than actually roasted in an oven. Although it is quicker to halve the peppers before grilling them, it is much better to keep them whole so that any juice released during cooking is contained inside the peppers. Place the peppers on a wire rack or grill pan and place under a hot grill for 10–12 minutes, turning them occasionally, until the skins have

blistered and blackened. Remove from the heat and cover with a clean dish towel; leave for a few minutes so that the steam helps to soften the skin and lift it away from the flesh. Holding the pepper in the dish towel, make a small hole in the bottom and gently squeeze the juices into a small bowl. Peel away the papery skin, then halve the pepper and remove the core and seeds.

SAFFRON

The most expensive spice in the world, saffron consists of the dark orange stigmas from flowering crocuses. The best saffron comes from La Mancha in Spain, although other countries do produce it. It has a fairly short shelf-life and should be infused in a little liquid such as wine or water before being used. Saffron is the key flavouring in the Spanish national dish, *paella*. It should be used sparingly as too much will give a slightly unpleasant, almost soapy flavour.

SALT COD

Salt cod comes in two basic types: fully dried and semi-dried. *Bacalao*, the Spanish salt cod, usually displayed as a whole fish, is fully dried. It needs a good 48 hours soaking in cold water to remove the salt and plump up the flesh, by which time it will be at least three times its original size. It is important to change the water every few hours.

Aromatic flavouring ingredients for tapas include (clockwise from the top): fresh garlic, paprika and saffron threads.

The second type of salt cod is semi-dried and can be found, in packets containing smaller pieces, in ethnic grocers. As it is less dry it only needs about 24 hours soaking and does not swell as much. It can be used in place of *bacalao* if necessary.

SCALLOPS

Most fishmongers sell scallops in their shells. Like clams, there are a number of different types and sizes, including the little queens. (These are ideal for grilling with brown butter, see page 36.)

To open a scallop, place it on a level surface with the flat shell uppermost. Slide a thin-bladed knife between the shells and cut the muscle which keeps the scallop closed. Lift off the top shell and pull out the grey frill around the scallop flesh. Carefully cut the meat out of the bottom shell, keeping the plump orange coral intact.

To cook the scallop, sear it briefly on a hot oiled griddle or heavy-based frying pan; if you intend returning it to the half-shell to serve, first rinse and dry the shell out thoroughly.

SHERRY

Sherry is a very valuable cooking ingredient – dry sherry can be used in place of white wine in any of the recipes here. It should be kept chilled and used soon after opening. Sweet sherries add a lovely flavour to many savoury dishes and are particularly good with meat dishes such as Chicken Livers in Sherry, see page 68.

SQUID

Squid can be bought ready cleaned and even cut into rings, but to prepare it yourself, gently pull the tentacles with the intestines attached away from the body. You may spot the ink sac with the intestines, this can be kept if desired, but the remainder should be discarded. Cut the edible tentacles off the head just above the eyes and remove, then pull out and discard the tough central beak. Peel the thin purple skin away from the white body and pull off the two fins. Thoroughly rinse the body tube, fins and tentacles.

Clockwise from bottom left: fresh mussels, clams, squid and salt cod.

COLD TAPAS

Cold tapas are a staple in most bars. Tasty snacks such as crunchy bread sticks, fried almonds or stuffed olives are often to be found lining the bar or tables in busy tascas. There is a wonderful selection of dishes in this chapter – choose from classic Marinated Olives, Sweet and Salty Beetroot Crisps, or melt-in-the-mouth Olive and Anchovy Bites. Many of the dishes can be made ahead of time, ready to be presented to unexpected guests, and are also good for packing into lunch boxes and picnic baskets.

Marinated Olives

For the best flavour, marinate the olives for at least 10 days and serve at room temperature.

INGREDIENTS

Serves 4
225g/8oz/1⅓ cups unpitted green olives
3 garlic cloves
5ml/1 tsp coriander seeds
2 small red chillies
2–3 thick slices of lemon, cut into pieces
1 thyme or rosemary sprig
75ml/5 tbsp white wine vinegar

> ——— COOK'S TIP ———
>
> For a change, use a mix of caraway and cumin seeds in place of the coriander.

1 Spread out the olives and garlic on a chopping board. Using a rolling pin, crack and flatten them slightly.

2 Crack the coriander seeds in a mortar with a pestle.

3 Mix the olives, garlic, coriander seeds, chillies, lemon pieces, herb sprig and wine vinegar in a large bowl. Toss well, then transfer the mixture to a clean glass jar. Pour in water to cover. Store in the fridge for at least 5 days before serving.

Salted Almonds

These crunchy salted nuts are at their best when fresh, so, if you can, cook them on the day you plan to eat them.

INGREDIENTS

Serves 2–4
115g/4oz/1 cup whole almonds in their skins
15ml/1 tbsp egg white, lightly beaten
2.5ml/½ tsp coarse sea salt

> ——— COOK'S TIP ———
>
> This traditional method of salt-roasting nuts gives a matt, dry-looking finish; if you want them to shine, tip the roasted nuts into a bowl, add 15ml/1 tbsp of olive oil and shake well to mix.

1 Preheat the oven to 180°C/350°F/ Gas 4. Spread out the almonds on a baking sheet and roast for about 20 minutes, until cracked and golden.

2 Mix the egg white and salt in a bowl, add the almonds and shake well to coat.

3 Tip out on to the baking sheet, give a shake to separate the nuts, then return them to the oven for 5 minutes, until they have dried. Leave until cold, then store in an airtight container until ready to serve.

Aubergine Purée

Serve this velvet-textured dip in the summertime, when there is a ready supply of firm, glossy aubergines to make it with, and crisp vegetables to serve it with.

INGREDIENTS

Serves 4

1 large aubergine
30ml/2 tbsp olive oil
2 garlic cloves, finely chopped
30ml/2 tbsp chopped fresh coriander
juice of ½ lemon
2.5ml/½ tsp cayenne pepper
salt and freshly ground black pepper
fresh coriander, to garnish

1 Preheat the oven to 200°C/400°F/ Gas 6. Place the aubergine on a baking sheet and cook for 30 minutes, until the skin is blackened and the aubergine is very soft.

2 Allow the aubergine to cool slightly. Cut it in half and use a tablespoon to scoop out the flesh into a bowl; discard the skin.

3 Mash the aubergine flesh using a fork to form a purée.

4 Stir in the olive oil, garlic, coriander and lemon juice, with enough cayenne, salt and pepper to suit your taste. Allow to cool and serve garnished with coriander.

COOK'S TIP

If preferred, the aubergine can be grilled for 20 minutes; turn it frequently.

Marinated Pimientos

Pimientos are simply cooked, skinned peppers. You can buy them in cans or jars, but they are much tastier when home-made.

INGREDIENTS

Serves 2–4
3 red peppers
2 small garlic cloves, crushed
45ml/3 tbsp chopped fresh parsley
15ml/1 tbsp sherry vinegar
30ml/2 tbsp olive oil
salt

1 Preheat the grill to high. Place the peppers on a baking sheet and grill for 8–12 minutes, turning occasionally, until the skins have blistered and blackened. Remove the peppers from the heat, cover with a clean dish towel and leave for 5 minutes so that the steam softens the skin.

2 Make a small cut in the bottom of each pepper and squeeze out the juice into a jug. Peel away the skin and cut both peppers in half. Remove and discard the core and seeds.

3 Using a sharp knife, cut each pepper in half lengthways into 1cm/½in wide strips and place them in a small bowl.

4 Whisk the garlic, parsley, vinegar and oil into the pepper juices. Add salt to taste. Pour over the pepper strips and toss well. Cover and chill, but, if possible, bring the peppers back to room temperature before serving.

Chick-pea Purée

INGREDIENTS

Serves 4
400g/14oz can chick-peas, drained
2 small garlic cloves, halved
60ml/4 tbsp fresh parsley leaves
60ml/4 tbsp olive oil
30ml/2 tbsp freshly squeezed
  lemon juice
salt and freshly ground black pepper
fresh parsley, to garnish

COOK'S TIP

For a change, try making this tapas dish with other canned beans such as cannellini beans or kidney beans.

1 Whizz the chick-peas, garlic and herbs in a food processor until finely chopped. With the motor running, slowly pour in the olive oil and lemon juice to make a thick purée.

2 Add salt and pepper to taste. Spoon the purée into a bowl, cover and chill until ready to serve, garnished with a sprig of parsley.

Sweet and Salty Beetroot Crisps

For a real treat, serve these brightly coloured crisps with a bowl of freshly made aïoli – the delicious garlicky mayonnaise.

INGREDIENTS

Serves 4
1 small fresh beetroot
caster sugar
fine salt and coarse sea salt
vegetable oil, for frying

1 Peel the beetroot and slice it very thinly, using a mandolin or a swivel-style vegetable peeler.

2 Lay the slices out on kitchen paper and sprinkle them lightly with sugar and salt.

COOK'S TIP

Beetroot crisps are particularly flavour-some, but other naturally sweet vegetables, such as carrot and sweet potato, also taste delicious when cooked like this. Make several different varieties, if you like, and serve them on a large flat platter or heaped in separate small bowls – they make ideal party nibbles.

3 Pour oil to a depth of 5cm/2in into a deep saucepan, then heat until a cube of bread turns golden in less than 1 minute. Cook the beetroot slices in batches for 1–2 minutes, until they float to the surface and turn golden brown around the edges. Drain the crisps on kitchen paper and leave to cool. Sprinkle with coarse sea salt before serving.

Pork Cracklings

These crisp savoury bites can be made well ahead, if you like. Store them in an airtight container for up to 2 weeks before serving.

INGREDIENTS

Serves 4
115g/4oz pork rind
vegetable oil, for frying
paprika
sea salt

COOK'S TIP

Although paprika can vary from fairly mild to hot, it isn't fiery hot – if you'd like to make these a little spicier, add a pinch of chilli powder to the paprika.

1 Using a sharp knife, cut the pork rind into strips about 1cm/½in wide and 2.5cm/1in long.

2 Pour vegetable oil to a depth of 2.5cm/1in into a deep heavy-based frying pan. Heat the oil until a cube of bread browns in 1 minute. Cook the strips of rind in the oil for 1–2 minutes, until puffed up and golden. Drain on kitchen paper and sprinkle with paprika and salt to taste. Serve hot or cold.

Banderillas

These miniature skewers are very popular in the tapas bars of northern Spain. They are generally made from a variety of pickled vegetables, but often also include cured or pickled fish, hard-boiled eggs, cooked prawns, tuna and cured meats. Be sure to eat this simple but classic *banderilla* in a single mouthful!

INGREDIENTS

Serves 4
12 small capers
12 drained anchovy fillets in oil
12 pitted black olives
12 cornichons or small gherkins
12 silverskin pickled onions

1 Place a caper at one end of each anchovy fillet and roll up.

2 Thread 1 caper-filled anchovy, 1 olive, 1 cornichon or gherkin and 1 pickled onion on to each of 12 cocktail sticks. Chill and serve.

COOK'S TIP

For a truly authentic *banderilla*, wrap a little square of coloured paper around the tip of the cocktail stick, so they resemble the bull-fighting dart that they are named after.

Marinated Anchovies

Make these at least 1 hour and up to 24 hours in advance. Fresh anchovies are tiny, so be prepared to spend time filleting them – the results will be worth the effort.

Ingredients

Serves 4
225g/8oz fresh anchovies
juice of 3 lemons
30ml/2 tbsp extra virgin olive oil
2 garlic cloves, finely chopped
15ml/1 tbsp chopped fresh parsley
flaked sea salt

1 Cut off the heads and tails from the anchovies, then split them open down one side.

2 Open each anchovy out flat and carefully lift out the bone.

3 Arrange the anchovies skin side down in a single layer on a plate. Pour over two-thirds of the lemon juice and sprinkle with the salt. Cover and leave for 1–24 hours, basting occasionally with the juices, until the flesh is white and no longer translucent.

4 Transfer the fish to a serving plate and drizzle over the olive oil and the remaining lemon juice. Scatter over the garlic and parsley, cover and chill until ready to serve.

Olive and Anchovy Bites

These melt-in-the-mouth morsels store very well; freeze them for up to 3 months or keep in an airtight container for up to 2 weeks before serving.

INGREDIENTS

Makes 40–45

115g/4oz/1 cup plain flour
115g/4oz/½ cup chilled butter
115g/4oz/1 cup finely grated cheese, such as Manchego, mature Cheddar or Gruyère
50g/2oz can anchovy fillets in oil, drained and roughly chopped
50g/2oz/⅓ cup pitted black olives, roughly chopped
2.5ml/½ tsp cayenne pepper
sea salt

COOK'S TIP

For a change, sprinkle the olive and anchovy bites with finely grated Parmesan cheese or dust lightly with cayenne pepper before baking.

1 Place the flour, butter, cheese, anchovies, olives and cayenne in a food processor and pulse until the mixture forms a firm dough.

2 Wrap the dough loosely in clear film. Chill for 20 minutes.

3 Preheat the oven to 200°C/400°F/ Gas 6. Roll out the dough thinly on a lightly floured surface.

4 Cut the dough into 5cm/2in wide strips, then cut across each strip diagonally, in alternate directions, to make triangles. Transfer to baking sheets and bake for 8–10 minutes until golden. Cool on a wire rack. Sprinkle with sea salt before serving.

Sesame Breadsticks

Breadsticks are one of the most versatile of tapas dishes. Try serving them with *banderillas* and a bowl of aïoli, or simply accompanied by a glass of red wine for dipping them into.

INGREDIENTS

Makes 30
225g/8oz/2 cups strong white flour
5ml/1 tsp salt
7g/¼ oz easy-blend dried yeast
30ml/2 tbsp sesame seeds
30ml/2 tbsp olive oil

COOK'S TIP

Breadsticks can be made with many different flavourings – try using fennel seeds, poppy seeds or finely grated Parmesan cheese instead of sesame seeds. They are best eaten fresh, so don't make them more than a day or two in advance. Store them in an airtight container until ready to eat.

1 Preheat the oven to 230°C/450°F/ Gas 8. Sift the flour into a bowl. Stir in the salt, yeast and sesame seeds and make a well in the centre.

2 Add the olive oil to the flour mixture and enough warm water to make a firm dough. Tip out the dough on to a lightly floured surface and knead for 5 – 10 minutes until smooth and elastic.

3 Rub a little oil on to the surface of the dough. Return it to the clean bowl and cover with a clean dish towel. Leave the dough to rise in a warm place for about 40 minutes, or until it has doubled in size.

4 Punch down the dough, then knead lightly until smooth. Pull off small balls of dough, then using your hands, roll out each ball on a lightly floured surface to a thin sausage about 25cm/10in long.

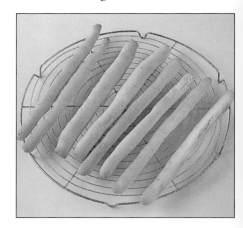

5 Place the breadsticks on baking sheets and bake for 15 minutes, until crisp and golden. Cool the breadsticks on a wire rack, then store them in an airtight container until ready to serve.

SEAFOOD TAPAS

Seafood plays a major role in Spanish cookery. Clams, scallops, mussels and the little chipirones (baby squid) make ideal, bite-sized tapas. Although the preparation of some seafood may be lengthy, it can all be done well ahead, and the actual cooking time is usually very short. In order to bring out the delicate flavour of the seafood, many of these tapas have been very simply prepared – pan-fried, grilled or steamed with little more than butter, garlic and a handful of fresh herbs, although there are the odd fancier exceptions such as the delicious Butterflied Prawns in Chocolate Sauce.

King Prawns in Sherry

INGREDIENTS

Serves 4

12 raw king prawns or tiger
  prawns, peeled
30ml/2 tbsp olive oil
30ml/2 tbsp sherry
few drops of Tabasco sauce
salt and freshly ground black pepper

1 Make a shallow cut down the back of each prawn, then pull out and discard the dark intestinal tract.

2 Heat the oil in a frying pan and fry the prawns for 2–3 minutes until pink. Pour over the sherry and season with Tabasco sauce, salt and pepper. Tip into a dish and serve immediately.

Sizzling Prawns

This dish works particularly well with tiny shrimps which can be eaten whole, but any type of prawns in the shell will be fine. Choose a small flameproof dish or frying pan that can be taken to the table for serving while the prawns are still sizzling.

INGREDIENTS

Serves 4

2 garlic cloves, halved
25g/1oz/2 tbsp butter
1 small red chilli, seeded and
  finely sliced
115g/4oz cooked prawns, in the shell
sea salt and coarsely ground
  black pepper
lime wedges, to serve

1 Rub the cut surfaces of the garlic cloves over the surface of a frying pan then throw them away. Add the butter to the pan and melt over a fairly high heat until it just begins to turn golden brown.

2 Toss in the chilli and prawns. Stir-fry for 1–2 minutes until heated through, then season to taste and serve with lime wedges to squeeze over.

COOK'S TIP

Wear gloves when handling chillies, or wash your hands thoroughly afterwards, as the juices can cause severe irritation to sensitive skin, especially around the eyes, nose or mouth.

Butterflied Prawns in Chocolate Sauce

Although the combination of flavours may seem odd, this is a truly delicious tapas. The use of bitter chocolate as a flavouring in savoury dishes is popular.

INGREDIENTS

Serves 4

8 large raw prawns, in the shell
15ml/1 tbsp seasoned flour
15ml/1 tbsp dry sherry
juice of 4 clementines or 1 large orange
15g/½oz unsweetened dark
    chocolate, chopped
30ml/2 tbsp olive oil
2 garlic cloves, finely chopped
2.5cm/1in piece fresh root ginger,
    finely chopped
1 small red chilli, seeded and chopped
salt and freshly ground black pepper

1 Peel the prawns, leaving just the tail sections intact. Make a shallow cut down the back of each prawn and carefully pull out and discard the dark intestinal tract. Turn over the prawns so that the undersides are uppermost, then carefully split them open from tail to top, using a small sharp knife, cutting almost, but not quite, through to the back.

2 Press the prawns down firmly to flatten them out. Coat with the seasoned flour and set aside.

3 Gently heat the sherry and clementine or orange juice in a small saucepan. When warm, remove from the heat and stir in the chopped chocolate until melted.

4 Heat the olive oil in a frying pan. Fry the garlic, ginger and chilli over a moderate heat for 2 minutes until golden. Remove with a slotted spoon and reserve. Add the prawns, cut-side down, to the pan; cook for 2–3 minutes until golden brown with pink edges. Turn and cook for a further 2 minutes.

5 Return the garlic mixture to the pan and pour over the chocolate sauce. Cook for 1 minute, turning the prawns to coat them in the glossy sauce. Season to taste and serve hot.

King Prawns in Crispy Batter

Serve with an oriental-style dipping sauce or offer a simple tomato sauce or lemon wedges.

INGREDIENTS

Serves 4

120ml/4fl oz/½ cup water
1 size 2 egg
115g/4oz/1 cup plain flour
5ml/1 tsp cayenne pepper
12 raw king prawns, in the shell
vegetable oil, for deep frying
lemon wedge and flat leaf parsley,
   to garnish

For the dipping sauce
30ml/2 tbsp soy sauce
30ml/2 tbsp dry sherry
10ml/2 tsp clear honey

1 In a large bowl, whisk the water with the egg. Add the flour and cayenne and whisk until smooth.

2 Carefully peel the prawns, leaving just the tail sections intact. Make a shallow cut down the back of each prawn, then pull out and discard the dark intestinal tract.

3 To make the dipping sauce, stir together the soy sauce, dry sherry and honey in a small bowl.

4 Heat the oil in a large saucepan or deep fryer, until a cube of bread browns in 1 minute.

5 Holding the prawns by their tails, dip them into the batter, one at a time shaking off any excess. Drop the prawns carefully into the oil and fry for 2–3 minutes until crisp and golden brown. Drain on kitchen paper and serve with the dipping sauce, garnished with a lemon wedge and parsley.

COOK'S TIP

If you have any batter left over, use it to coat thin strips of vegetable such as sweet potato, beetroot, carrot or pepper, or use small broccoli florets or whole baby spinach leaves. Deep-fry until golden.

Seafood Salad

INGREDIENTS

Serves 6
115g/4oz prepared squid rings
1 large carrot
6 crisp lettuce leaves, torn into pieces
10cm/4in piece cucumber,
  finely diced
12 fresh mussels, in their
  shells, steamed
100g/4oz cooked, peeled prawns
15ml/1 tbsp drained capers

For the dressing
30ml/2 tbsp freshly squeezed
  lemon juice
45ml/3 tbsp olive oil
15ml/1 tbsp chopped fresh parsley
sea salt and freshly ground black pepper

--- COOK'S TIP ---

For a change, use any type of cooked seafood or fish in this salad – try steamed clams or cockles, prawns in their shells or cubes of firm fish.

1 Place the squid rings in a metal sieve or vegetable steamer. Place over a saucepan of simmering water, cover and steam for 2–3 minutes until the squid just turns white. Cool under cold running water and drain on kitchen paper.

2 Using a swivel-style vegetable peeler, cut the carrot into wafer thin ribbons. Place the lettuce on a serving plate. Scatter over the carrot ribbons, followed by the diced cucumber.

3 Arrange the mussels, prawns and squid rings over the salad and scatter the capers over the top.

4 Whisk the dressing ingredients in a small bowl and drizzle over the salad. Chill before serving.

Baked Clams

This simple, fresh-tasting tapas also works very well with mussels.

INGREDIENTS

Serves 4
400g/14oz can chopped tomatoes
1 red onion, chopped
60ml/4 tbsp snipped fresh chives
450g/1lb small fresh clams
15–30ml/1–2 tbsp olive oil
salt and freshly ground black pepper
sniped chives, to garnish

--- COOK'S TIP ---

Cooked this way, the onions are fairly crunchy – if you prefer, fry them first.

1 Preheat the oven to 200°C/400°F/ Gas 6. Tip the tomatoes into a bowl and stir in the chopped onion and chives, with salt and pepper to taste. Transfer to a heatproof dish, cover with foil and bake for 10 minutes.

2 Arrange the clams, joint side down, in the tomato mixture. Drizzle over the olive oil and return to the oven for 5–10 minutes until the clams have opened. Discard any clams that remain closed, then scatter over the chives and serve at once.

Spiced Clams

Turmeric is not usually used with clams, but combines with chilli powder and fresh ginger to create a delicious dish.

INGREDIENTS

Serves 4
1 small onion, cut into thin wedges
1 celery stick, sliced
2 garlic cloves, chopped
2.5cm/1in piece fresh root
  ginger, grated
30ml/2 tbsp olive oil
5ml/1 tsp chilli powder
5ml/1 tsp ground turmeric
30ml/2 tbsp chopped fresh parsley
450g/1lb fresh baby clams
30ml/2 tbsp dry white wine
salt and freshly ground black pepper
celery leaves, to garnish

1 Place the onion, celery, garlic and ginger in a saucepan, add the oil, spices and parsley and stir-fry for about 5 minutes.

COOK'S TIP

It is very important that the paste is cooked for a full 5 minutes or the finished dish will have the harsh taste of raw spices.

2 Add the clams to the pan and cook for 2 minutes.

3 Pour in the wine, then cover and cook gently for 2–3 minutes, shaking the pan occasionally, until all the shells have opened. Add plenty of salt and pepper to taste. Discard any clams whose shells remain closed, then serve at once in bowls, garnished with the celery leaves.

Steamed Mussels with Bacon and Beer

The idea of combining mussels, bacon and beer actually comes from Belgium. Surprisingly, these ingredients go remarkably well together and they make a fabulous tapas dish.

INGREDIENTS

Serves 6
15ml/1 tbsp olive oil
1 small onion, chopped
2 garlic cloves, finely chopped
4 rindless smoked streaky bacon
  rashers, roughly chopped
500g/1¼lb prepared small mussels
75ml/5 tbsp blond beer or lager
5ml/1 tsp chopped fresh thyme
coarsely ground black pepper
sprigs of thyme, to garnish

1 Heat the oil in a frying pan and fry the onion, garlic and bacon over a high heat for 5 minutes until golden.

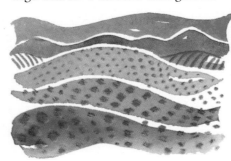

2 Add the mussels, beer or lager and thyme, with pepper to taste. Cover tightly and steam for 3–5 minutes until all the mussels have opened. Spoon into serving dishes, discarding any mussels that remain closed. Serve hot, garnished with thyme sprigs.

Grilled Mussels with Parsley and Parmesan

This is sure to become one of your all-time favourite tapas – as the mussels are grilling, they release an irresistible aroma. When you make them at home, don't be surprised if they are devoured the moment they are ready!

INGREDIENTS

Serves 4

450g/1lb fresh mussels
45ml/3 tbsp water
15ml/1 tbsp melted butter
15ml/1 tbsp olive oil
45ml/3 tbsp freshly grated
  Parmesan cheese
30ml/2 tbsp chopped fresh parsley
2 garlic cloves, finely chopped
2.5ml/½ tsp coarsely ground black
  pepper

1 Scrub the mussels thoroughly, scraping off any barnacles with a round-bladed knife and pulling out the gritty beards. Sharply tap any open mussels and discard any that fail to close.

2 Place the mussels and water in a large pan. Cover and steam for 5 minutes, or until the mussels have opened.

3 Drain the mussels, discarding any that remain closed. Snap the top shell off each, leaving the mussel still attached to the bottom shell.

4 Balance the shells in a flameproof dish, packing them closely together so they stay level.

--- COOK'S TIP ---

If you can't get fresh mussels, shelled frozen mussels will work well. Thaw and drain, then place in four individual heat-proof dishes. Top with the parsley mixture and grill for the same time. Serve the mussels with teaspoons and offer plenty of bread to mop up the juices.

5 Preheat the grill to high. In a small bowl, mix together the melted butter, olive oil, Parmesan, parsley, garlic and black pepper.

6 Place a small amount of the cheese mixture on top of each mussel.

7 Grill for 2–3 minutes or until the mussels are sizzling and golden. Serve the mussels in their shells, but remember to give the guests napkins to wipe the juices off their chins!

Grilled Scallops with Brown Butter

This is a very striking dish as the scallops are served on the half shell, still sizzling from the grill. Reserve it for a special occasion, when you want to impress!

INGREDIENTS

Serves 4
50g/2oz/¼ cup unsalted
  butter, diced
8 scallops, prepared on the half shell
15ml/1 tbsp chopped fresh parsley
salt and freshly ground black pepper
4 lemon wedges, to serve

1 Preheat the grill to high. Melt the butter in a small saucepan over a moderate heat until it is pale golden brown. Remove the pan from the heat immediately; the butter must not be allowed to burn.

2 Arrange the scallop shells in a single layer in a flameproof serving dish or a shallow roasting tin. Brush a little of the brown butter over the scallops and grill for 4 minutes – it will not be necessary to turn them.

3 Pour over the remaining brown butter, then sprinkle a little salt and pepper and the parsley over the top. Serve at once, with lemon wedges.

> ——— COOK'S TIP ———
>
> If you can't get hold of scallops in their shells, you can use shelled fresh scallops if you cook them on the day of purchase.

Fried Squid

The squid is simply dusted in flour and dipped in egg before being fried so the coating is light, and does not mask the flavour.

INGREDIENTS

Serves 4
115g/4oz prepared squid, cut
  into rings
30ml/2 tbsp seasoned flour
1 egg
30ml/2 tbsp milk
olive oil, for frying
sea salt
lemon wedges, to serve

> ——— COOK'S TIP ———
>
> For a crisper coating, dust the rings in flour, then dip them in batter instead of this simple egg and flour coating.

1 Toss the squid rings in the seasoned flour in a bowl or strong plastic bag. Beat the egg and milk together in a shallow bowl. Heat the oil in a heavy-based frying pan.

2 Dip the floured squid rings one at a time into the egg mixture, shaking off any excess liquid. Add to the hot oil, in batches if necessary, and fry for 2–3 minutes on each side until golden.

3 Drain the fried squid on kitchen paper, then sprinkle with salt. Transfer to a small warm plate and serve with the lemon wedges.

Paella Croquettes

Paella is probably Spain's most famous dish and here it is used for a tasty fried tapas. In this recipe, the paella is cooked from scratch, but you could, of course, use leftover paella instead.

INGREDIENTS

Serves 4

pinch of saffron threads
150ml/¼ pint/⅔ cup white wine
30ml/2 tbsp olive oil
1 small onion, finely chopped
1 garlic clove, finely chopped
115g/4oz/⅔ cup risotto rice
300ml/½ pint/1¼ cups hot chicken stock
50g/2oz cooked prawns, peeled, deveined and roughly chopped
50g/2oz cooked chicken, roughly chopped
50g/2oz/⅓ cup petits pois, thawed if frozen
30ml/2 tbsp freshly grated Parmesan cheese
1 egg, beaten
30ml/2 tbsp milk
75g/3oz/1½ cups fresh white breadcrumbs
vegetable or olive oil, for frying
salt and freshly ground black pepper
flat leaf parsley, to garnish

1 Stir the saffron into the wine in a small bowl; set aside.

2 Heat the oil in a heavy-based saucepan and gently fry the onion and garlic for 5 minutes until softened. Stir in the rice and cook for 1 minute.

3 Keeping the heat fairly high, add the wine and saffron mixture to the pan, stirring until it is all absorbed. Gradually add the stock, stirring until all the liquid has been absorbed and the rice is cooked – this should take about 20 minutes.

COOK'S TIP

When making paella, it's very improtant to use a good quality short grain rice. Italian risotto rice, sometimes labelled arborio or carnaroli, works very well.

4 Stir in the prawns, chicken, petits pois and freshly grated Parmesan. Season to taste with salt and pepper. Allow to cool slightly, then use two tablespoons to shape the mixture into 16 small lozenges.

5 Mix the egg and milk in a shallow bowl. Spread out the breadcrumbs on a sheet of foil. Dip the croquettes in the egg mixture, then coat them in the breadcrumbs.

6 Heat the oil in a large frying pan. Shallow fry the croquettes for 4–5 minutes until crisp and golden brown. Drain on kitchen paper and serve hot, garnished with a sprig of flat leaf parsley.

FISH TAPAS

This is a rather summery selection of recipes including Grilled Sardines, which are wonderful cooked on a barbecue, and Salt-cured Salmon, which is sliced wafer-thin and served chilled with aïoli. Another European favourite, whitebait, is given a special Spanish feel when fried until crisp and served with a sherry salsa. Also covered in this chapter is the typical Spanish fish bacalao (salt cod) – used here to make two delicious tapas, bite-size fish cakes and basil-flavoured fritters.

Monkfish Parcels

INGREDIENTS

Serves 4

175g/6oz/1½ cups strong plain flour
2 eggs
115g/4oz skinless monkfish fillet, diced
grated rind of 1 lemon
1 garlic clove, chopped
1 small red chilli, seeded and sliced
45ml/3 tbsp chopped fresh parsley
30ml/2 tbsp single cream

For the tomato oil

2 tomatoes, peeled, seeded and
    finely diced
45ml/3 tbsp extra virgin olive oil
30ml/1 tbsp fresh lemon juice
salt and freshly ground black pepper

COOK'S TIP

If the dough is sticky, sprinkle a little flour
into the food processor bowl.

1 Place the flour, eggs and 2.5ml/ ½ tsp salt in a food processor; pulse until the mixture forms a soft dough. Knead for 2−3 minutes then wrap in clear film. Chill for 20 minutes.

2 Place the monkfish, lemon rind, garlic, chilli and parsley in the clean food processor; process until very finely chopped. Add the cream, with plenty of salt and pepper and whizz again to form a very thick purée.

3 Make the tomato oil by stirring the diced tomato with the olive oil and lemon juice in a bowl. Add salt to taste. Cover and chill.

4 Roll out the dough on a lightly floured surface and cut out 32 rounds, using a 4cm/1½in plain cutter. Divide the filling among half the rounds, then cover with the remaining rounds. Pinch the edges tightly to seal, trying to exclude as much air as possible.

5 Bring a large saucepan of water to simmering point and poach the parcels, in batches, for 2−3 minutes or until they rise to the surface. Drain and serve hot, drizzled with the tomato oil.

Salt Cod Fishcakes with Aïoli

Bite-size fish cakes, dipped in a rich garlic mayonnaise, are irresistible. Start these in good time, as the salt cod needs lengthy soaking.

INGREDIENTS

Serves 6

450g/1lb potatoes, peeled and cubed
115g/4oz salt cod, soaked in cold water for 48 hours
15ml/1 tbsp olive oil
1 small onion, finely chopped
2 garlic cloves, finely chopped
30ml/2 tbsp chopped fresh parsley
1 egg, beaten
Tabasco or chilli sauce
plain flour, for dusting
vegetable oil, for frying
salt and freshly ground black pepper
flat leaf parsley and lemon wedges, to garnish
aïoli, to serve

COOK'S TIP

Try making these with drained canned fish, such as salmon or tuna.

1 Cook the potatoes in a saucepan of boiling water for 10–12 minutes until tender. Drain well, then mash until smooth. Set aside.

2 Place the cod in a frying pan, add water to cover and bring to the boil. Drain the fish, then remove the skin and bones. Using a fork, break the flesh into small pieces.

3 Heat the olive oil in a small saucepan and cook the onion and garlic for 5 minutes until softened.

4 In a large bowl, mix together the mashed potato, flaked fish, fried onion mixture and parsley. Bind with the egg, then add salt, pepper and Tabasco or chilli sauce to taste. With floured hands, shape the mixture into 18 small balls.

5 Flatten the balls slightly and place on a large floured plate. Chill for about 15 minutes.

6 Heat 1cm/½in vegetable oil in a large frying pan. Cook the fish cakes for 3–4 minutes on each side until golden. Drain on kitchen paper and serve hot, with the aïoli, garnished with parsley and lemon wedges.

Salt Cod Fritters

Start this recipe ahead of time as the salt cod must be soaked for 2 days before it is used.

INGREDIENTS

Serves 4 – 6
115g/4oz/1 cup self-raising flour
2.5ml/½ tsp salt
1 large egg
60ml/4 tbsp milk
115g/4oz salt cod, soaked in water for 48 hours
4 spring onions, finely chopped
small handful of basil leaves, roughly torn
5ml/1 tsp coarsely ground black pepper
olive oil, for frying

1 Sift the flour into a bowl and stir in the salt. Whisk in the egg and milk to make a thick batter.

2 Drain the salt cod. Remove the skin and bones, then flake the flesh. Stir it into the batter with the spring onions, basil and pepper.

3 Heat 1cm/½in olive oil in a frying pan. Place spoonfuls of the mixture into the pan.

4 Cook for 2 – 3 minutes on each side until puffed and golden. Drain on kitchen paper and serve hot.

COOK'S TIP

For an extra light result, let the batter rest for 20 minutes before stirring in the spring onions, basil and pepper.

Cod with Potato and Mustard Seeds

INGREDIENTS

Serves 4

30ml/2 tbsp olive oil
5ml/1 tsp mustard seeds
1 large potato, cubed
2 slices of serrano ham, shredded
1 onion, thinly sliced
2 garlic cloves, thinly sliced
1 red chilli, seeded and sliced
115g/4oz skinless, boneless cod, cubed
120ml/4fl oz/½ cup vegetable stock
50g/2oz/½ cup grated tasty cheese,
     such as Manchego or Cheddar
salt and freshly ground black pepper

--- COOK'S TIP ---

For a crisp topping, substitute half the
cheese with wholemeal breadcrumbs.

1 Heat the oil in a heavy-based
frying pan. Add the mustard seeds.
Cook for a minute or two until the
seeds begin to pop and splutter, then
add the potato, ham and onion.

2 Cook, stirring regularly for about
10–15 minutes, until the potatoes
are brown and almost tender.

3 Add the garlic and chilli and cook
for 2 minutes more.

4 Stir in the cod cubes and cook for
2–3 minutes until white, then add
the stock and plenty of salt and pepper.
Cover the pan and cook for 5 minutes,
until the fish is just cooked and the
potatoes are tender.

5 Transfer the mixture to a flameproof dish. Sprinkle over the
grated cheese and place under a hot
grill for about 2–3 minutes until the
cheese is golden and bubbling.

Fried Whitebait with Sherry Salsa

INGREDIENTS

Serves 4
225g/8oz whitebait, thawed if frozen
30ml/2 tbsp seasoned flour
60ml/4 tbsp olive oil
60ml/4 tbsp vegetable oil

For the salsa
1 shallot, finely chopped
2 garlic cloves, finely chopped
4 ripe tomatoes, roughly chopped
1 small red chilli, seeded and finely
  chopped
30ml/2 tbsp olive oil
60ml/4 tbsp sweet sherry
30–45ml/2–3 tbsp chopped fresh herbs,
  such as basil, parsley or coriander
25g/1oz/½ cup fresh white
  breadcrumbs
salt and freshly ground black pepper

1 To make the salsa, place the shallot, garlic, tomatoes, chilli and oil in a pan. Cover with a lid and cook gently for 10 minutes.

2 Pour in the sherry and add salt and pepper to taste. Stir in the herbs and breadcrumbs, then cover and keep hot until the whitebait are ready.

3 Wash the whitebait thoroughly, drain well, then dust in the seasoned flour to coat. Heat both oils together in a heavy-based frying pan and cook the fish in batches until crisp and golden. Drain on kitchen paper and keep warm in a low oven until all the fish are cooked. Serve at once with the salsa.

Crispy Fish Balls

You can use any white fish to make these crispy balls. Cod, haddock and monkfish fillet all work well.

INGREDIENTS

Serves 6
1 egg
pinch of saffron threads
2 garlic cloves, roughly chopped
45ml/3 tbsp parsley leaves
225g/8oz white fish, skinned, boned
  and cubed
75g/3oz white bread,
  crusts removed
60ml/4 tbsp seasoned flour
vegetable oil, for frying
salt and freshly ground black pepper
lemon wedges, mayonnaise and
  cocktail sticks, to serve

1 Beat the egg and saffron threads together in a cup, then set aside for 5 minutes.

2 In a food processor, whizz the garlic and parsley together until finely chopped. Add the fish and bread and whizz until well blended. Scrape the fish mixture into a bowl and stir in the egg and saffron. Season with plenty of salt and pepper.

3 Shape the mixture into 24 small balls. Spread out the seasoned flour in a shallow dish and coat the balls on all sides.

4 Heat the oil in a deep frying pan. Fry the fish balls, in batches if necessary, until crisp and golden, shaking the pan to keep them moving. Drain on kitchen paper and serve immediately with lemon wedges. Offer a small bowl of mayonnaise for dipping and cocktail sticks for spearing.

Grilled Sardines

Fresh sardines have plenty of flavour, so they are at their best when cooked simply.

INGREDIENTS

Serves 4

8 sardines, about 50g/2oz each
sea salt
2 lemons, halved

1 Gut the sardines, but leave on the heads and tails. Slash each of the sardines' sides diagonally three times.

2 Preheat the grill to high. Place the sardines on a rack and sprinkle with sea salt. Grill for 4 minutes on each side until the flesh is cooked and the skin is blistered and a little charred.

3 Transfer to a serving dish and serve at once with the lemon halves to squeeze over.

Salt-cured Salmon

INGREDIENTS

Serves 10

50g/2oz/¼ cup sea salt
45ml/3 tbsp caster sugar
5ml/1 tsp chilli powder
5ml/1 tsp coarsely ground
  black pepper
45ml/3 tbsp chopped fresh coriander
2 x 250g/9oz salmon fillets
flat leaf parsley, to garnish
aïoli, to serve

—————— COOK'S TIP ——————

Make the most of the left-over salmon skin by turning it into delicious crunchy strips: after slicing the salt-cured salmon, scrape any remaining fish off the skin and discard. Cut the skin into 1cm/½in wide strips. Fry for 1 minute in hot oil until crisp and browned. Drain on kitchen paper; allow to cool. Serve as a garnish for the salt-cured salmon or as a tapas dish in its own right.

3 Chill for 48 hours, turning every 8 hours or so and basting with the liquid that forms in the dish.

1 In a bowl mix together the salt, sugar, chilli powder, pepper and coriander. Rub the mixture into the flesh of each salmon fillet.

2 Place one of the fillets, skin-side down in a shallow glass dish. Place the other fillet on top, with the skin side up. Cover with foil then place a weight on top.

4 Drain the salmon well and transfer to a board. Using a sharp knife, slice it diagonally into wafer thin slices. Arrange on plates and garnish with sprigs of parsley. Serve with the aïoli.

MEAT AND POULTRY TAPAS

This chapter includes a mixture of authentic tapas, such as Chorizo in Red Wine, and Spicy Meatballs, along with delicious contemporary dishes, such as Chicken with Lemon and Garlic, and Ham and Cheese Toasts, which are made using traditional ingredients. Sausages, including morcilla, fresh spicy sausages and cured chorizo sausage, all feature strongly, with recipes for the popular tapas dish, Fried Black Pudding, and a robust Sausage Stew.

Pastry-wrapped Chorizo Puffs

These flaky pastry puffs, filled with spicy chorizo sausage and grated cheese, make a perfect accompaniment to a glass of cold sherry or beer. You can use any type of hard cheese for the puffs, but for best results choose a mild variety, as the chorizo has plenty of flavour.

INGREDIENTS

Serves 8

225g/8oz puff pastry, thawed
    if frozen
115g/4oz cured chorizo sausage,
    chopped
50g/2oz/½ cup grated cheese
1 small egg, beaten
5ml/1 tsp paprika

1 Roll out the pastry thinly on a floured surface. Using a 7.5cm/3in cutter, stamp out as many rounds as possible, then re-roll the trimmings, if necessary, and stamp out more rounds to make 16 in all.

2 Preheat the oven to 220°C/450°F/ Gas 7. Put the chopped chorizo sausage and grated cheese in a bowl and toss together lightly.

3 Lay one of the pastry rounds on the palm of your hand and place a little of the chorizo mixture across the centre.

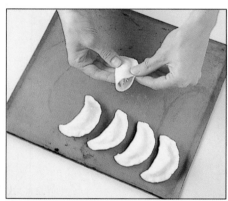

4 Using your other hand, pinch the edges of the pastry together along the top to seal, as when making a miniature pastie. Repeat the process with the remaining rounds to make 16 puffs in all.

--- COOK'S TIP ---

Prepare the chorizo puffs a day or two ahead, if you like. Chill them without the glaze, wrapped in a plastic bag, until ready to bake, then allow them to come back to room temperature while you preheat the oven. Glaze before baking.

5 Place the pastries on a non-stick baking sheet and brush lightly with the beaten egg. Using a small sieve or tea strainer, dust the tops lightly with a little of the paprika.

6 Bake the pastries for 10–12 minutes, until puffed and golden brown. Transfer the pastries to a wire rack and leave to cool for 5 minutes, then serve warm, dusted with the rest of the paprika.

Chorizo in Red Wine

This simple dish is flamed just before serving. If you wish, use small chorizo sausages and leave them whole. Provide cocktail sticks for spearing the chorizo.

INGREDIENTS

Serves 4
225g/8oz cured chorizo sausage
90ml/6 tbsp red wine
30ml/2 tbsp brandy
chopped fresh parsley, to garnish

COOK'S TIP

After cooking, the chorizo can be cooled, then chilled for up to 24 hours.

1 Prick the chorizo sausage(s) in several places with a fork and place in a saucepan with the wine. Bring to the boil, lower the heat, then cover and simmer gently for 15 minutes. Remove from the heat and leave to cool in the covered pan for 2 hours.

2 Remove the chorizo sausage(s) from the pan and reserve the wine.

3 Cut the chorizo sausage(s) into 1cm/½ in slices.

4 Heat the chorizo in a heavy-based frying pan, then pour over the brandy and light very carefully with a match. When the flames have died down, add the reserved wine and cook for 2–3 minutes until piping hot. Serve garnished with chopped parsley.

Fried Black Pudding

Black pudding (*morcilla*) is a very popular tapas dish. In Spain the sausage is often home-made.

INGREDIENTS

Serves 4
15ml/1 tbsp olive oil
1 onion, thinly sliced
2 garlic cloves, thinly sliced
5ml/1 tsp dried oregano or marjoram
5ml/1 tsp paprika
225g/8oz black pudding, cut in 12
  thick slices
1 small French stick, sliced into
  12 rounds
30ml/2 tbsp dry sherry
sugar, to taste
salt and freshly ground black pepper
chopped oregano, to garnish

1 Heat the oil in a large frying pan and fry the onion, garlic, oregano and paprika for 7–8 minutes until the onion is softened and golden.

2 Add the black pudding slices, raise the heat and cook for 3 minutes on each side until crisp.

3 Arrange the rounds of bread on a large serving plate and top each with a slice of black pudding. Stir the sherry into the mixture remaining in the frying pan, with sugar to taste. Heat, swirling around until bubbling, then season with salt and pepper.

4 Spoon a little of the onion mixture on top of each slice of black pudding. Scatter over the oregano and serve immediately.

COOK'S TIP

If you do find real *morcilla*, which is usually flavoured with spices and herbs (including paprika, garlic and marjoram), serve it neat: simply fry the slices in olive oil and use to top little rounds of bread.

Sausage Stew

This robust tapas dish is very good served with a glass of beer.

INGREDIENTS

Serves 4

15ml/1 tbsp olive oil
1 onion, chopped
2 garlic cloves, finely chopped
1 carrot, chopped
4 fresh spicy sausages
150ml/¼ pint/⅔ cup tomato juice
15ml/1 tbsp brandy
1.5ml/¼ tsp Tabasco sauce
5ml/1 tsp sugar
salt and freshly ground black pepper
30ml/2 tbsp chopped fresh coriander,
   to garnish

1 Heat the oil in a large saucepan. Cook the onion, garlic, carrot and sausages for 10 minutes, stirring occasionally until evenly browned.

2 Stir in the tomato juice, brandy, Tabasco and sugar, with salt and pepper to taste. Cover and simmer for 25 minutes until the sausages are cooked through and the sauce has thickened. Serve at once, garnished with chopped coriander.

Stewed Beans and Pork

Fabada is a classic Spanish stew which takes its name from a type of white bean. It always contains black pudding (*morcilla*) and chorizo sausage and usually takes a good 2 hours to prepare. Here is a simple, speedy version that serves very well as tapas.

INGREDIENTS

Serves 4

15ml/1 tbsp olive oil
175g/6oz belly pork, rind removed
   and diced
115g/4oz cured chorizo sausage, diced
1 onion, chopped
2 garlic cloves, finely chopped
1 large tomato, roughly chopped
1.5ml/¼ tsp dried chilli flakes
400g/14oz can cannellini
   beans, drained
150ml/¼ pint/⅔ cup chicken stock
salt and freshly ground black pepper
flat leaf parsley, to garnish

1 Heat the oil in a large frying pan and fry the pork, chorizo, onion and garlic for 5–10 minutes until the onion has softened and browned. Add the tomato and chilli flakes and cook for 1 minute more.

2 Stir in the beans and stock. Bring to the boil, lower the heat, cover and simmer for 15–20 minutes until the pork is cooked through. Add salt and pepper to taste and serve, garnished with parsley.

COOK'S TIP

If preferred, smoked gammon can be used in place of belly pork in this recipe. Although it isn't quite as authentic, the meat is a lot less fatty and it adds a good smokey flavour.

Cheese and Ham Potato Patties

These soft patties can be served hot or cold – for a real treat, top each with a fried quail's egg.

INGREDIENTS

Serves 4

500g/1¼lb potatoes, peeled and cubed
25g/1oz/2 tbsp butter
50g/2oz/¼ cup grated cheese, such as
  Manchego or mature Cheddar
4 slices of serrano ham, chopped
50g/2oz/½ cup plain flour
oil for greasing
salt and freshly ground black pepper

1 Cook the potatoes in a saucepan of boiling, lightly salted water for 10–15 minutes until tender. Drain well and mash with the butter and cheese until smooth.

2 Stir in the ham and flour with plenty of salt and pepper. Shape the mixture into eight rounds, each about 1cm/½in thick.

3 Lightly oil a griddle or heavy-based frying pan and cook the patties for 4–5 minutes on each side until golden brown. Drain on kitchen paper and serve at once.

COOK'S TIP

The patties have a very fluffy, soft centre, so take care when turning them over. If preferred, brush them with oil and cook them under a moderately hot grill, turning them halfway through cooking.

Egg-fried Ham Sandwiches

For a new slant on the toasted sandwich, serve these tasty snacks with their golden egg coating. Vary the filling – cheese works particularly well.

INGREDIENTS

Serves 2

2 slices of serrano ham
2 large slices of white bread,
 crusts removed
1 egg
30ml/2 tbsp milk
30ml/2 tbsp olive oil
coarse sea salt and freshly ground
 black pepper

COOK'S TIP

The longer you soak the sandwich, the more egg mixture will be absorbed and the lighter and fluffier will be the result – 15 minutes is ideal.

1 Lay both slices of ham on one of the slices of bread. Sprinkle with pepper, then cover with the other slice of bread to make a sandwich.

2 Beat the egg and milk together in a shallow dish. Cut the sandwich into four squares and place in the egg mixture, turning once or twice until all the liquid has been absorbed.

3 Heat the oil in a frying pan. Cook the sandwiches for 3–4 minutes on each side until puffed up and golden brown. Remove with a fish slice and drain on kitchen paper. Sprinkle lightly with sea salt and serve hot.

Spicy Meatballs

These meatballs are delicious served piping hot with chilli sauce on the side so guests can add as much heat as they like.

INGREDIENTS

Serves 6

115g/4oz fresh spicy sausages
115g/4oz minced beef
2 shallots, finely chopped
2 garlic cloves, finely chopped
75g/3oz/1½ cups fresh white
    breadcrumbs
1 egg, beaten
30ml/2 tbsp chopped fresh parsley, plus
    extra to garnish
15ml/1 tbsp olive oil
salt and freshly ground black pepper
Tabasco sauce or other hot chilli sauce,
    to serve

1 Remove the skins from the sausages and place the sausagemeat in a small mixing bowl.

COOK'S TIP

If you like, you can make the meatballs up to a day in advance, then cover and chill them until ready to cook.

2 Add the minced beef, shallots, garlic, breadcrumbs, beaten egg and parsley, with plenty of salt and pepper. Mix well, then shape into 18 small balls.

3 Heat the olive oil in a large frying pan and cook the meatballs, in batches if necessary, for about 15 – 20 minutes, stirring regularly until evenly browned and cooked through.

4 Transfer the meatballs to a warm plate and sprinkle with chopped parsley. Serve with chilli sauce. Offer cocktail sticks for spearing.

Meatballs in Tomato Sauce

Serve this traditional tapas dish with crusty bread and a robust red wine or, for a light meal for two, with a bowl of steaming pasta tossed in olive oil.

INGREDIENTS

Serves 4
225g/8oz minced beef or lamb
4 spring onions, thinly sliced
2 garlic cloves, finely chopped
30ml/2 tbsp freshly grated Parmesan
10ml/2 tsp fresh thyme leaves
15ml/1 tbsp olive oil
3 tomatoes, chopped
30ml/2 tbsp red or dry white wine
10ml/2 tsp chopped fresh rosemary
pinch of sugar
salt and freshly ground black pepper
fresh thyme, to garnish

1 Place the minced beef or lamb in a bowl. Add the spring onions, garlic, Parmesan and thyme and plenty of salt and pepper.

2 Mix well, then shape the mixture into 12 small firm balls.

3 Heat the olive oil in a large frying pan and cook the meatballs for 5 minutes, turning frequently until evenly browned.

4 Add the chopped tomatoes, wine, rosemary and sugar, with salt and pepper to taste. Cover and cook gently for 15 minutes until the tomatoes are pulpy and the meatballs are cooked. Serve hot, garnished with thyme.

Spicy Chicken Wings

These deliciously sticky bites will appeal to adults and children alike, although younger eaters might prefer a little less chilli.

INGREDIENTS

Serves 4
8 plump chicken wings
2 large garlic cloves, cut into slivers
15ml/1 tbsp olive oil
15ml/1 tbsp paprika
5ml/1 tsp chilli powder
5ml/1 tsp dried oregano
5ml/1 tsp salt
5ml/1 tsp ground black pepper
lime wedges, to serve

— COOK'S TIP —

Chunks of chicken breast and small thighs may also be cooked in this way.

1 Using a small sharp knife, make one or two cuts in the skin of each chicken wing and carefully slide a sliver of garlic under the skin. Brush the wings with the olive oil.

2 In a large bowl, stir together the paprika, chilli powder, oregano, salt and pepper. Add the chicken wings and toss together until very lightly coated in the mixture.

3 Grill or barbecue the chicken wings for 15 minutes until they are cooked through with a blackened, crispy skin. Serve with lime wedges to squeeze over.

Chicken with Lemon and Garlic

Extremely easy to cook and delicious to eat, serve this succulent tapas dish with fried potatoes and aïoli.

INGREDIENTS

Serves 4
225g/8oz skinless chicken breast fillets
30ml/2 tbsp olive oil
1 shallot, finely chopped
4 garlic cloves, finely chopped
5ml/1 tsp paprika
juice of 1 lemon
30ml/2 tbsp chopped fresh parsley
salt and freshly ground black pepper
flat leaf parsley, to garnish
lemon wedges, to serve

1 Sandwich the chicken breasts between two sheets of clear film or greaseproof paper. Bat out with a rolling pin until the fillets are about 5mm/¼in thick.

— COOK'S TIP —

For a variation on this dish, try using strips of turkey breast or pork.

2 Cut the chicken into strips about 1cm/½in wide. Heat the oil in a large frying pan. Stir-fry the chicken strips with the shallot, garlic and paprika over a high heat for about 3 minutes until lightly browned and cooked through. Add the lemon juice and parsley with salt and pepper to taste. Serve hot with lemon wedges, garnished with flat leaf parsley.

Chicken Liver Pâté

This rich-tasting, smooth pâté will keep in the fridge for 3–4 days. Serve with thick slices of hot toast or warm bread – a rustic olive oil bread such as ciabatta is the ideal choice.

INGREDIENTS

Serves 8

115g/4oz chicken livers, thawed if
   frozen, trimmed
1 small garlic clove, chopped
15ml/1 tbsp sherry
30ml/2 tbsp brandy
50g/2oz/¼ cup butter, melted
1.5ml/¼ tsp salt
fresh herbs and black peppercorns,
   to garnish
hot toast and warm bread, to serve

1 Preheat the oven to 150°C/300°F/ Gas 2. Place the chicken livers and chopped garlic in a food processor and whizz until smooth.

2 With the motor running, gradually add the sherry, brandy, melted butter and salt.

3 Pour the mixture into two 7.5cm/ 3in ramekins and cover with foil.

4 Place the ramekins in a small roasting tin and pour in boiling water until it comes halfway up the sides of the ramekins.

5 Carefully transfer the tin to the oven and bake for 20 minutes. Allow to cool to room temperature, then remove the ramekins from the tin and chill until ready to serve. Serve the pâté with toast or bread, garnished with herbs and peppercorns.

Chicken Croquettes

This recipe comes from Rebato's, a tapas bar in London. The chef there makes croquettes with a number of flavourings; this version uses chicken.

INGREDIENTS

Serves 4

25g/1oz/2 tbsp butter
25g/1oz/¼ cup plain flour
150ml/¼ pint/⅔ cup milk
15ml/1 tbsp olive oil
1 boneless chicken breast with skin, about 75g/3oz, diced
1 garlic clove, finely chopped
1 small egg, beaten
50g/2oz/1 cup fresh white breadcrumbs
vegetable oil for deep frying
salt and freshly ground black pepper
flat leaf parsley, to garnish
lemon wedges, to serve

1 Melt the butter in a small saucepan. Add the flour and cook gently, stirring, for 1 minute. Gradually beat in the milk to make a smooth, very thick sauce. Cover with a lid and remove from the heat.

2 Heat the oil in a frying pan and cook the chicken with the garlic for 5 minutes, until the chicken is lightly browned and cooked through.

3 Tip the contents of the frying pan into a food processor and process until finely chopped. Stir into the sauce. Add plenty of salt and pepper to taste, then leave to cool completely.

4 Shape into eight small sausages, then dip each in egg and then breadcrumbs. Deep fry in hot oil for 4 minutes until crisp and golden. Drain on kitchen paper and serve with lemon wedges, garnished with flat leaf parsley.

Chicken Livers in Sherry

This dish makes an excellent
addition to any tapas spread.
Serve with crusty bread.

INGREDIENTS

Serves 4
225g/8oz chicken livers, thawed if
  frozen, trimmed
1 small onion
2 small garlic cloves
15ml/1 tbsp olive oil
5ml/1 tsp fresh thyme leaves
30ml/2 tbsp sweet sherry
30ml/2 tbsp soured or double cream
salt and freshly ground black pepper
fresh thyme, to garnish

1 Trim any green spots and sinews
from the chicken livers; set aside
while you prepare the onion and garlic.

2 Finely chop the onion and garlic
using a sharp knife.

3 Heat the oil in a frying pan and fry
the onion, garlic, chicken livers
and thyme for 3 minutes.

4 Stir in the sherry and cook gently
for 1 minute. Add the soured or
double cream and cook over a low heat
for 1–2 minutes more. Stir in salt and
pepper to taste and serve at once,
garnished with thyme.

MEAT AND POULTRY TAPAS 69

Sweet Crust Lamb

These little noisettes are just big enough for two mouthfuls, so are ideal for tapas. If you would prefer something a little more substantial, small lamb cutlets or chops can be prepared in the same way.

INGREDIENTS

Serves 8

175g/6oz tender lamb fillet, sliced into
  1cm/½in rounds
5ml/1 tsp English mustard
30ml/2 tbsp light muscovado sugar
salt and freshly ground black pepper
cocktail sticks, to serve

1 Preheat the grill to high. Sprinkle the rounds of lamb generously with salt and pepper and grill on one side for 2 minutes until well browned.

2 Remove the grill pan from the grill. Turn the lamb rounds over and spread with the mustard.

3 Sprinkle the sugar evenly over the lamb rounds, then return the grill pan to the grill.

4 Cook the lamb for 2–3 minutes more, until the sugar has melted, but the lamb is still pink in the centre. Serve with cocktail sticks for spearing.

— COOK'S TIP —

Watch the lamb carefully while it is grilling, as the sugar may burn if cooked for more than a few minutes.

Skewered Lamb with Red Onion Salsa

This summery tapas dish is ideal for outdoor eating, although, if the weather fails, the skewers can be cooked under a conventional grill. The simple salsa makes a refreshing accompaniment – make sure that you use a mild-flavoured red onion which is fresh and crisp, and a tomato which is ripe and full of flavour.

INGREDIENTS

Serves 4
225g/8oz lean lamb, cubed
2.5ml/½ tsp ground cumin
5ml/1 tsp ground paprika
15ml/1 tbsp olive oil
salt and freshly ground black pepper

For the salsa
1 red onion, very thinly sliced
1 large tomato, seeded and chopped
15ml/1 tbsp red wine vinegar
3–4 fresh basil or mint leaves,
  roughly torn
small mint leaves, to garnish

1 Place the lamb in a bowl with the cumin, paprika, olive oil and plenty of salt and pepper. Toss well until the lamb is coated with spices.

2 Cover the bowl with clear film and leave in a cool place for several hours, or in the fridge overnight, so that the lamb absorbs the spicy flavours.

3 Spear the lamb cubes on four small skewers – if using wooden skewers, soak them first in cold water for at least 30 minutes to prevent them burning.

4 To make the salsa, put the sliced onion, tomato, vinegar and basil or mint leaves in a small bowl and stir together until thoroughly blended. Season to taste with salt, garnish with mint, then set aside while you cook the skewered lamb.

5 Cook the skewered lamb over hot coals or under a preheated grill for about 5–10 minutes, turning the skewers frequently, until the lamb is well browned but still slightly pink in the centre. Serve hot, with the salsa.

COOK'S TIP

For an alternative to the red onion salsa, stir chopped fresh mint or basil and a little lemon juice into a small pot of Greek-style yogurt. Drizzle the mixture over the cooked kebabs before serving.

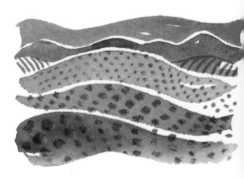

VEGETARIAN AND VEGETABLE TAPAS

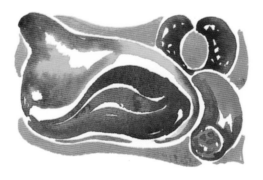

When presenting a selection of tapas, it is important to balance out the meat and seafood dishes with a few vegetable tapas — many of which are the more well known, such as tortilla and patatas bravas. Although most fresh vegetables are available all year round, try to choose vegetables when in the peak of the season as they are not only less expensive but also far more flavoursome — very important for dishes such as Tomato and Garlic Bread. This chapter also includes other non-meat dishes such as Fried Cheese and Fried Dough Balls.

Mini Rice Omelettes

INGREDIENTS

Serves 4

30ml/2 tbsp olive oil
115g/4oz/1 cup cooked white rice
1 potato, grated
4 spring onions, thinly sliced
1 garlic clove, finely chopped
15ml/1 tbsp chopped fresh parsley
3 eggs, beaten
salt and freshy ground black pepper

1 Heat half the olive oil in a large frying pan and stir-fry the rice, with the potato, spring onions and garlic, over a high heat for 3 minutes until golden.

2 Tip the rice and vegetable mixture into a bowl and stir in the parsley and eggs, with plenty of salt and pepper. Mix well.

3 Heat the remaining oil in the frying pan and drop in large spoonfuls of the rice mixture, leaving room for spreading. Cook the omelettes for 1–2 minutes on one side then flip over and cook the other side.

4 Drain the omelettes on kitchen paper and keep hot while cooking the remaining mixture to make 8 small omelettes in all. Serve hot.

Fried Cheese

This tapas works very well with Cheddar, mozzarella and, surprisingly, goat's cheese, but the best is Manchego. This dish doesn't like to wait around, so fill your kitchen with friends who are ready to eat the cubes as soon as they're out of the pan.

INGREDIENTS

Serves 4

225g/8oz firm cheese
30ml/2 tbsp seasoned flour
1 egg, beaten
60ml/4 tbsp chopped fresh dill
vegetable oil, for deep frying
cocktail sticks, to serve

1 Cut the cheese into 2cm/¾in cubes. Roll the cubes in seasoned flour to coat them evenly.

--- COOK'S TIP ---

Test the temperature with one cube of cheese before you cook them all. If the oil is not hot enough, the cheese will take too long to crisp and the centre is likely to ooze out completely.

2 Beat the egg and dill together, then dip the cubes into the mixture to coat. Heat 2.5cm/1in oil in a heavy-based frying pan. Fry the cubes for 1–2 minutes on each side until golden.

3 Remove the cubes with a slotted spoon, drain on kitchen paper and serve immediately, with cocktail sticks on hand for spearing.

Cheese Puff Balls

INGREDIENTS

Serves 4

50g/2oz/4 tbsp butter, cubed
1.5ml/¼ tsp salt
250ml/8fl oz/1 cup water
115g/4oz/1 cup plain flour
2 whole eggs, plus 1 yolk
2.5ml/½ tsp English mustard powder
2.5ml/½ tsp cayenne pepper
50g/2oz/½ cup finely grated well-
  flavoured cheese, such as Manchego
  or Cheddar

— COOK'S TIP —

Stir snipped chives, smoked salmon or ham
into soft cheese and use as a filling for cold
puffs.

1 Preheat the oven to 220°C/425°F/
Gas 7. Place the butter, salt and
water in a pan. Bring to the boil.

2 Sift the flour on to a sheet of
greaseproof paper, then tip it all
into the boiling liquid and stir it in
very quickly.

3 Beat the mixture with a wooden
spoon to form a thick paste that
leaves the sides of the pan clean.
Remove the pan from the heat.

4 Beat in the eggs and yolk, one at a
time, then add the mustard,
cayenne and cheese.

5 Place teaspoonfuls of the mixture
on to a non-stick baking sheet and
bake for 10 minutes. Lower the oven
temperature to 180°C/ 350°F/Gas 4
and cook for a further 15 minutes until
well browned. Serve immediately or
cool on a wire rack and serve cold.

Tomato and Garlic Bread

A basket of warm, crusty, garlic-flavoured bread is a compulsory addition to any tapas table.

INGREDIENTS

Serves 4–6

4 large ripe tomatoes,
   roughly chopped
2 garlic cloves, roughly chopped
1.5ml/¼ tsp sea salt
grated rind and juice of ½ lemon
5ml/1 tsp soft light brown sugar
1 flat loaf of bread, such as ciabatta
30ml/2 tbsp olive oil
freshly ground black pepper

1 Preheat the oven to 200°C/400°F/ Gas 6. Place the tomatoes, garlic, salt, lemon rind and brown sugar in a small saucepan. Cover and cook gently for 5 minutes until the tomatoes have released their juices and the mixture is quite watery.

2 Split the loaf in half horizontally, then cut each half widthways into 2–3 pieces. Place on a baking sheet and bake for 5–8 minutes until hot, crisp and golden brown.

3 While the bread is baking, stir the lemon juice and olive oil into the tomato mixture. Cook uncovered for 8 minutes more, until the mixture is thick and pulpy.

4 Spread the tomato mixture on the hot bread, sprinkle with pepper and serve at once.

Fried Dough Balls with Fiery Salsa

These crunchy dough balls are accompanied by a hot and spicy tomato salsa. Serve them with a juicy tomato salad, if you prefer.

INGREDIENTS

Serves 10

450g/1lb/4 cups strong white flour
5ml/1 tsp easy-blend dried yeast
5ml/1 tsp salt
30ml/2 tbsp chopped fresh parsley
2 garlic cloves, finely chopped
30ml/2 tbsp olive oil, plus extra
  for greasing
vegetable oil, for frying

For the salsa

6 hot red chillies, seeded and
  roughly chopped
1 onion, roughly chopped
2 garlic cloves, quartered
2.5cm/1in piece of root ginger,
  roughly chopped
450g/1lb tomatoes, roughly chopped
30ml/2 tbsp olive oil
pinch of sugar
salt and freshly ground black pepper

1 Sift the flour into a large bowl. Stir in the yeast and salt and make a well in the centre. Add the parsley, garlic, olive oil and enough warm water to make a firm dough.

2 Gather the dough in the bowl together then tip out on to a lightly floured surface or board. Knead for about 10 minutes, until the dough feels very smooth and elastic.

3 Rub a little oil into the surface of the dough. Return it to the clean bowl, cover with clear film or a clean dish towel and leave in a warm place to rise for about 1 hour, or until doubled in bulk.

4 Meanwhile, make the salsa. Combine the chillies, onion, garlic and ginger in a food processor and whizz together until very finely chopped. Add the tomatoes and olive oil and process until smooth.

5 Sieve the mixture into a saucepan. Add sugar, salt and pepper to taste and simmer gently for 15 minutes. Do not allow the salsa to boil.

6 Roll the dough into about 40 balls. Shallow fry in batches in hot oil for 4–5 minutes until crisp and golden. Drain on kitchen paper and serve hot, with the fiery salsa in a separate bowl for dipping.

COOK'S TIP

These dough balls can be deep-fried for 3–4 minutes or baked at 200°C/400°F/Gas 6 for 15–20 minutes.

Grilled Pepper Tartlets

INGREDIENTS

Serves 4

175g/6oz/1½ cups plain flour
pinch of salt
75g/3oz/6 tbsp chilled butter, diced
30−45ml/2−3 tbsp water
1 red pepper, seeded and quartered
1 yellow pepper, seeded and quartered
60ml/4 tbsp double cream
1 egg
15ml/1 tbsp freshly grated
   Parmesan cheese
salt and freshly ground black pepper

COOK'S TIP

For a change, try filling the pastry cases
with strips of grilled aubergine mixed with
sun-dried tomato, or strips of grilled
courgette mixed with toasted pine nuts.

1 Sift the flour and salt into a bowl.
Add the butter and rub it in with
your fingertips until the mixture
resembles fine breadcrumbs. Stir in
enough of the water to make a firm,
not sticky, dough.

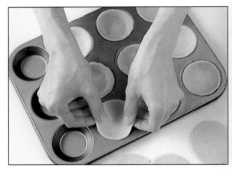

2 Preheat the oven to 200°C/400°F/
Gas 6. Roll the dough out thinly
on a lightly floured surface and line
12 individual moulds or a 12-hole
tartlet tin. Prick the bases with a fork
and fill the pastry cases with crumpled
foil. Bake for 10 minutes.

3 Meanwhile, place the peppers
skin-side up on a baking sheet and
grill for 10 minutes until the skin is
blistered and blackened. Cover with a
dish towel and leave for 5 minutes,
then peel away the skin.

4 Cut each piece of pepper
lengthways into very thin strips.
Remove the foil from the pastry cases
and divide the pepper strips among
the pastry cases.

5 Whisk the cream and egg in a
bowl. Add plenty of salt and
pepper and pour over the peppers.
Sprinkle the Parmesan over each filled
tartlet and bake for 15−20 minutes
until firm and golden brown. Cool for
2 minutes before removing from the
moulds and transferring to wire racks;
serve warm or cold.

Baked Peppers and Tomatoes

Make sure there is a basket of warm bread on hand so that none of the delicious juices from this dish are wasted.

INGREDIENTS

Serves 8
2 red peppers
2 yellow peppers
1 red onion, sliced
2 garlic cloves, halved
6 plum tomatoes, quartered
50g/2oz/¼ cup black olives
5ml/1 tsp soft light brown sugar
45ml/3 tbsp sherry
3–4 rosemary sprigs
30ml/2 tbsp olive oil
salt and freshly ground black pepper

1 Seed the red and yellow peppers, then cut each into 12 strips.

2 Preheat the oven to 200°C/400°F/ Gas 6. Place the peppers, onion, garlic, tomatoes and olives in a large roasting tin. Sprinkle over the sugar, then pour over the sherry. Season well, cover with foil and bake for 45 minutes.

3 Remove the foil from the tin and stir the mixture well. Add the rosemary sprigs.

4 Drizzle over the olive oil. Return the tin to the oven for a further 30 minutes until the vegetables are tender. Serve hot.

COOK'S TIP

Use four or five well-flavoured beefsteak tomatoes instead of plum tomatoes if you prefer. Cut them into thick wedges instead of quarters.

Fried Spinach with Garlic

Serve this dish warm, or chill and squeeze over a little lemon juice just before eating.

INGREDIENTS

Serves 4
2 tomatoes
450g/1lb spinach
2 garlic cloves, very thinly sliced
45ml/3 tbsp olive oil
salt and grated nutmeg

——— COOK'S TIP ———

There are a number of easy ways to remove the skin from a tomato – if you don't have a gas stove, place the tomatoes under a hot grill for 1 minute on each side, or plunge them into a saucepan of boiling water for 1 minute.

1 Spear each tomato in turn on a fork and hold in the flame of a gas burner for a few seconds on each side until the skin blisters (see Cook's Tip). Peel off the skin, cut the tomatoes in half, scoop out the seeds and discard.

2 Chop the flesh of both tomatoes into 5mm/¼ in pieces.

3 Wash the spinach well. Place it in a large saucepan with the chopped tomatoes and the garlic. Cover and steam for 5 minutes until dark green and wilted. Drain well.

4 Heat the olive oil in a large frying pan. Gently fry the spinach mixture, tossing and turning until it is glossy and hot. Do not let the garlic darken, or it will taste bitter. Season the spinach and serve, sprinkled with a little grated nutmeg.

Charred Artichokes with Lemon Oil Dip

INGREDIENTS

Serves 4

15ml/1 tbsp lemon juice or white
    wine vinegar
2 globe artichokes, trimmed
12 garlic cloves, unpeeled
45ml/3 tbsp olive oil
1 lemon
45ml/3 tbsp olive oil
sea salt
sprigs of flat leaf parsley,
    to garnish

1 Preheat the oven to 200°C/400°F/ Gas 6. Add the lemon juice or vinegar to a bowl of cold water. Cut each artichoke lengthways into wedges. Pull the hairy choke out from the centre of each wedge, then drop them into the acidulated water.

2 Drain the artichoke wedges and place in a roasting tin with the garlic. Add the oil and toss well to coat. Sprinkle with salt and roast for 40 minutes, stirring once or twice, until they are tender and a little charred.

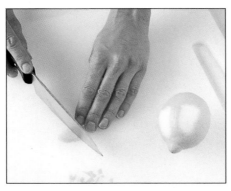

3 Meanwhile, make the dip. Using a small, sharp knife thinly pare away two strips of rind from the lemon. Lay the strips on a board and carefully scrape away any remaining pith. Place the rind in a small pan with water to cover. Bring to the boil, then simmer for 5 minutes. Drain the rind, refresh it in cold water, then chop it roughly. Set it aside.

4 Arrange the cooked artichokes on a serving plate and set aside to cool for 5 minutes. Using the back of a fork, gently flatten the garlic cloves so that the flesh squeezes out of the skins. Transfer the garlic flesh to a bowl, mash to a purée then add the lemon rind. Squeeze the juice from the lemon, then, using the fork, whisk the remaining olive oil and the lemon juice into the garlic mixture. Serve the artichokes warm with the lemon dip.

COOK'S TIP

Artichokes are usually boiled, but dry-heat cooking also works very well. If you can get young artichokes, try roasting them over a barbecue.

Broad Beans with Bacon

This is a classic combination, however, for a change, or if you'd like to serve this dish to vegetarians, you can omit the chopped bacon and substitute the same quantity of drained sun-dried tomatoes in oil – it will be equally delicious.

INGREDIENTS

Serves 4
30ml/2 tbsp olive oil
1 small onion, finely chopped
1 garlic clove, finely chopped
50g/2oz rindless smoked streaky bacon, roughly chopped
225g/8oz broad beans, thawed if frozen
5ml/1 tsp paprika
15ml/1 tbsp sweet sherry
salt and freshly ground black pepper

1 Heat the oil in a saucepan and fry the onion, garlic and bacon over a high heat for 5 minutes until softenend and browned.

2 Add the beans and paprika and stir-fry for 1 minute. Add the sherry, cover and cook for 5–10 minutes until the beans are tender. Add salt and pepper to taste.

— COOK'S TIP —

If you have time, remove the dull skins from the broad beans to reveal the bright green beans beneath.

Garlic Mushrooms

Provide crusty bread to mop up the creamy cooking liquid.

INGREDIENTS

Serves 4
25g/1oz/2 tbsp butter
225g/8oz large flat mushrooms, sliced
4 garlic cloves, thinly sliced
30ml/2 tbsp chopped fresh parsley
30ml/2 tbsp double cream
salt and freshly ground black pepper

1 Heat the butter in a large frying pan. Add the mushrooms and garlic and cook for 5 minutes until the mushrooms are tender and have released their juices.

2 Stir in the parsley and cream, season to taste and cook for a further 1–2 minutes until piping hot.

— COOK'S TIP —

For added variety, flavour and texture, use a mixture of mushrooms, such as chestnut mushrooms, oyster mushrooms and tiny button mushrooms.

Mushrooms Stuffed with Walnuts and Tomatoes

INGREDIENTS

Serves 4

50g/2oz/½ cup walnuts, roughly
  chopped
4 sun-dried tomatoes in oil, drained
115g/4oz/½ cup soft cheese
12 closed cup mushrooms, about
  225g/8oz, stalks removed
15ml/1 tbsp butter
50g/2oz/½ cup grated Manchego or
  Cheddar cheese
salt and coarsely ground black pepper
flat leaf parsley, to garnish

COOK'S TIP

For a delicious variation, use only half the
filling, coat the mushrooms in flour, egg
and breadcrumbs and deep-fry until crisp.

1 Place the chopped walnuts in a
small frying pan. Shake the pan
over a gentle heat for 3–5 minutes
until the walnuts are golden brown.
Chop the sun-dried tomatoes.

2 Tip the walnuts into a bowl and
stir in the sun-dried tomatoes and
soft cheese, with salt and pepper to
taste. Fill the mushroom caps with
the mixture.

3 Preheat the grill to medium-high.
Melt the butter in a flameproof
dish large enough to hold all the
mushrooms in a single layer. Add the
mushrooms, stuffing-side up, then grill
gently for about 7 minutes.

4 Sprinkle the mushrooms with the
cheese and then grill for 5 minutes
more, until the cheese is bubbling and
the mushrooms are tender. Serve hot,
garnished with flat leaf parsley.

Russian Salad

This colourful cold salad is a tapas bar staple.

INGREDIENTS

Serves 4

8 new potatoes, scrubbed
  and quartered
1 large carrot, diced
115g/4oz fine green beans, cut into
  2cm/³⁄₄in lengths
75g/3oz/³⁄₄ cup peas
½ Spanish onion, chopped
4 cornichons or small gherkins, sliced
1 small red pepper, seeded and diced
50g/2oz/¹⁄₃ cup pitted black olives
15ml/1 tbsp capers
60–90ml/4–6 tbsp aïoli or
  mayonnaise
15ml/1 tbsp freshly squeezed
  lemon juice
30ml/2 tbsp chopped fresh dill
salt and freshly ground black pepper
fresh dill, to garnish

— COOK'S TIP —

For a sweeter flavour, roast and skin the pepper before adding it to the salad.

1 Cook the potatoes and diced carrot in a saucepan of boiling lightly salted water for 5–8 minutes until almost tender. Add the beans and peas to the pan and cook for 2 minutes more, or until all the vegetables are tender. Drain well.

2 Tip the cooked vegetables into a large bowl. Add the onion, cornichons or gherkins, red pepper, olives and capers. Stir the aïoli or mayonnaise and lemon juice together.

3 Add most of the dressing and the dill to the vegetables with plenty of freshly ground black pepper. Toss well to lightly coat the vegetables. Chill until ready to serve, then drizzle with the remaining dressing and garnish with the dill.

Stewed Aubergines

INGREDIENTS

Serves 4

60–90ml/4–6 tbsp olive oil
1 large aubergine, sliced into 1cm/
½ in rounds
2 shallots, thinly sliced
4 tomatoes, quartered
2 garlic cloves, thinly sliced
60ml/4 tbsp red wine
30ml/2 tbsp chopped fresh parsley, plus
extra to garnish
salt and freshly ground black pepper

--- COOK'S TIP ---

For a tasty variation, spoon the cooked mixture into a flameproof dish, sprinkle with grated cheese and grill for 5 minutes, until bubbling and golden.

1 Heat 15ml/1 tbsp of the oil in a large frying pan. Cook the aubergine slices in batches (adding more oil as necessary, but reserving 15ml/1 tbsp), until golden brown. Drain the slices, cut them into strips about 1cm/½ in wide, and set aside.

2 Heat the reserved 15ml/1 tbsp of oil in a saucepan and cook the shallots for 5 minutes until golden. Add the aubergine strips with the tomatoes, garlic and wine. Season to taste. Cover and simmer for 30 minutes. Stir in the parsley, check the seasoning and serve, sprinkled with chopped parsley.

Courgette Fritters

Serve these crisp fritters with a dipping sauce such as aïoli, tomato sauce, Sherry Salsa or Fiery Salsa.

INGREDIENTS

Serves 4

2 courgettes
25g/1oz/¼ cup seasoned flour
2 eggs, beaten
30ml/2 tbsp milk
vegetable oil, for frying
coarse sea salt

1 Cut the courgettes on the diagonal into slices about 5mm/¼ in thick. Toss the slices in the seasoned flour in a strong plastic bag. Beat together the egg and milk in a small bowl. Heat 1cm/½ in oil in a frying pan.

2 Shake off the excess flour from the courgette slices. Dip them one at a time into the egg mixture, until they are well coated.

3 Shallow fry the fritters in the hot oil for 1–2 minutes on each side until crisp and golden. Drain on kitchen paper and serve, lightly sprinkled with sea salt.

Grilled Asparagus with Salt-cured Ham

Serve this tapas when asparagus is plentiful and not too pricey.

INGREDIENTS

Serves 4
6 slices of serrano ham
12 asparagus spears
15ml/1 tbsp olive oil
sea salt and coarsely ground black
    pepper

COOK'S TIP

If you can't find serrano ham, use Italian prosciutto or Portuguese *presunto*.

1 Preheat the grill to high. Halve each slice of ham lengthways and wrap one half around each of the asparagus spears.

2 Brush the ham and asparagus lightly with oil and sprinkle with salt and pepper. Place on the grill rack. Grill for 5–6 minutes, turning frequently, until the asparagus is tender but still firm. Serve at once.

Braised Buttery Cabbage with Chorizo

This dish is equally delicious without the chorizo sausage, so just omit it when serving this to vegetarian guests.

INGREDIENTS

Serves 4
50g/2oz/¼ cup butter
1 tsp caraway seeds
225g/8oz green cabbage, shredded
2 garlic cloves, finely chopped
50g/2oz cured chorizo sausage,
    roughly chopped
60ml/4 tbsp dry sherry or white wine
salt and freshly ground black pepper

COOK'S TIP

Smoked bacon makes a good substitute for chorizo sausage in this recipe. Add it to the pan after the caraway seeds and cook for a few minutes before adding the cabbage.

1 Melt the butter in a frying pan, add the caraway seeds and cook for 1 minute. Add the cabbage to the pan with the garlic and chorizo. Stir-fry for 5 minutes until the cabbage is tender.

2 Add the sherry or wine and plenty of salt and pepper. Cover the pan and cook for 15–20 minutes until the cabbage is tender. Check the seasoning and serve.

Fried Potatoes with Aïoli

Aïoli is a Catalan speciality which began life as a mixture of garlic, salt and olive oil, pounded together with a pestle in a mortar. Nowadays, it is usually made in a food processor and is more like garlic mayonnaise.

INGREDIENTS

Serves 4

4 potatoes, cut into 8 wedges each
vegetable oil, for deep frying
coarse sea salt

For the aïoli

1 large egg yolk, at room
  temperature
5ml/1 tsp white wine vinegar
75ml/5 tbsp olive oil
75ml/5 tbsp sunflower oil
4 garlic cloves, crushed

1 Make the aïoli. Place the egg yolk and vinegar in a food processor. With the motor running, add the olive oil, about 10ml/2 tsp at a time.

2 When all the olive oil has been added, add the sunflower oil in the same way, until the aïoli resembles a thick mayonnaise. If it is too thick, add a little more vinegar. Stir in the garlic and salt to taste. Cover and chill.

3 Heat the oil in a saucepan until a cube of bread turns golden in 60 seconds. Add the potatoes and cook for 7 minutes until pale golden.

4 Remove the potato wedges from the pan and drain on kitchen paper. Raise the heat of the oil slightly – it should be hot enough to brown a cube of bread in 30 seconds. Return the potatoes to the pan and cook for 2–3 minutes until golden brown. Drain on kitchen paper and sprinkle with salt. Serve hot with the aïoli.

COOK'S TIP

This aïoli recipe has equal quantities of olive oil and sunflower oil, but aïoli can be made with 3 parts sunflower oil to 1 part olive oil for a milder flavour. If made solely with olive oil, the finished aïoli will have a waxy appearance and strong, slightly bitter flavour.

Spicy Potatoes

Spicy potatoes, *patatas picantes,* are among the most popular tapas dishes in Spain, where they are sometimes described as *patatas bravas* (wild potatoes). There are many variations of this classic: boiled new potatoes or large wedges of fried potato may be used, but they are perhaps best simply roasted as in this recipe.

INGREDIENTS

Serves 2–4
225g/8oz small new potatoes
15ml/1 tbsp olive oil
5ml/1 tsp paprika
5ml/1 tsp chilli powder
2.5ml/½ tsp ground cumin
2.5ml/½ tsp salt
flat leaf parsley, to garnish

1 Preheat the oven to 200°C/400°F/ Gas 6. Prick the skin of each potato in several places with a fork, then place them in a bowl.

2 Add the olive oil, paprika, chilli, cumin and salt and toss well.

3 Transfer the potatoes to a roasting tin and bake for 40 minutes.

— COOK'S TIP —

This dish is delicious served with tomato sauce or Fiery Salsa – provide small forks for dipping.

4 Occasionally during cooking, remove the potatoes from the oven and turn them. Serve hot, garnished with flat leaf parsley.

Artichoke Rice Cakes with Melting Manchego

For a really impressive tapas, serve these rice cakes topped with aïoli and Salt-cured Salmon.

INGREDIENTS

Serves 6

1 globe artichoke
50g/2oz/¼ cup butter
1 small onion, finely chopped
1 garlic clove, finely chopped
115g/4oz/⅔ cup risotto rice
450ml/¾ pint/scant 2 cups hot
   chicken stock
50g/2oz/¼ cup freshly grated
   Parmesan cheese
150g/5oz Manchego cheese, very
   finely diced
45–60ml/3–4 tbsp fine cornmeal
olive oil for frying
salt and freshly ground black pepper
flat leaf parsley, to garnish

1 Remove the stalk, leaves and choke to leave just the heart of the artichoke; chop the heart finely.

2 Melt the butter in a saucepan and gently fry the chopped artichoke heart, onion and garlic for 5 minutes until softened. Stir in the rice and cook for about 1 minute.

3 Keeping the heat fairly high, gradually add the stock, stirring constantly until all the liquid has been absorbed and the rice is cooked – this should take about 20 minutes. Season well, then stir in the Parmesan. Transfer to a bowl. Leave to cool, then cover and chill for at least 2 hours.

4 Spoon about 15ml/1 tbsp of the mixture into the palm of one hand, flatten slightly, and place a few pieces of diced cheese in the centre. Shape the rice around the cheese to make a small ball. Flatten slightly then roll in the cornmeal, shaking off any excess. Repeat with the remaining mixture to make about 12 cakes.

5 Shallow fry in hot olive oil for 4–5 minutes until the rice cakes are crisp and golden brown. Drain on kitchen paper and serve hot, garnished with flat leaf parsley.

— COOK'S TIP —

Fresh Parmesan should be piquant, grainy and not so hard that it is difficult to grate.

Classic Potato Tortilla

A traditional Spanish tortilla contains potatoes and onions. Other ingredients can be added to the basic egg mixture, but it is generally accepted that the classic tortilla cannot be improved.

INGREDIENTS

Serves 6

450g/1lb small waxy potatoes, peeled
1 Spanish onion
45ml/3 tbsp vegetable oil
4 eggs
salt and freshly ground black pepper
flat leaf parsley, to garnish

1 Cut the potatoes into thin slices and the onions into rings.

2 Heat 30ml/2 tbsp of the oil in a 20cm/8in heavy-based frying pan. Add the potatoes and the onions and cook over a low heat for about 10 minutes until the potatoes are just tender. Remove from the heat.

3 In a large bowl, beat together the eggs with a little salt and pepper. Stir in the sliced potatoes and onion.

4 Heat the remaining oil in the frying pan and pour in the potato mixture. Cook very gently for 5–8 minutes until the mixture is almost set.

5 Place a large plate upside-down over the pan, invert the tortilla on to the plate and then slide it back into the pan. Cook for 2 or 3 minutes more, until the underside of the tortilla is golden brown. Cut into wedges and serve, garnished with flat leaf parsley.

Index